JAN 1 1 2016

DISCOVER EARTH SCIENCE

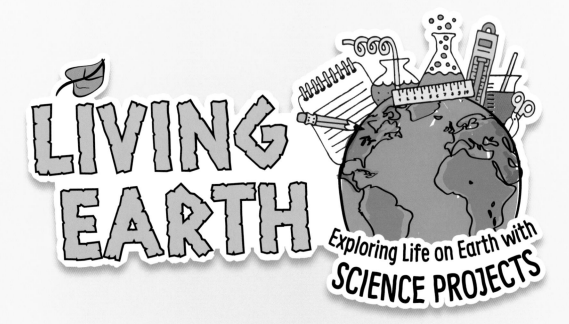

LIVING EARTH

Exploring Life on Earth with SCIENCE PROJECTS

by Suzanne Garbe

Consultant:
Daniel S. Jones, Research Associate
Department of Earth Sciences & BioTechnology Institute
University of Minnesota

CAPSTONE PRESS
a capstone imprint

Fact Finders Books are published by Capstone Press,
1710 Roe Crest Drive, North Mankato, Minnesota 56003
www.capstonepub.com

Library of Congress Cataloging-in-Publication Data
Garbe, Suzanne.
  Living earth : exploring life on earth with science projects / by Suzanne Garbe.
      pages cm.—(Fact finders. Discover earth science.)
  Includes bibliographical references and index.
  Summary: "Illustrated instructions for experiments pertaining to life on Earth,
including photosynthesis, bacteria, minerals, and fossils"—Provided by publisher.
  ISBN 978-1-4914-4816-8 (library binding)
  ISBN 978-1-4914-4915-8 (eBook PDF)
1. Earth science projects—Juvenile literature. I. Title.
  QE29.G374 2016
  550.78—dc23   2014047993

Editorial Credits
Alesha Sullivan, editor; Sarah Bennett, designer; Kelly Garvin, media researcher;
Lori Barbeau, production specialist

Photo Credits
Capstone Press/Karon Dubke, 7, 9, 12, 13, 15, 18–19, 22, 23, 25, 28; Shutterstock: Evan
Lorne, 10–11, focal point, 8, Jezper, 26–27, Jorg Hackemann, 24, Krivosheev Vitaly, 6–7,
Konstantnin, 14, Marcio Jose Bastos Silva, 16–17, Natursports, 19 (top right), otsphoto,
4–5, R.L.Hausdorf, 20–21, sittitap, cover, snapgalleria, 6 (bottom right), Stephen Tucker,
29, Studio_G, 27 (inset)

Design Elements: Shutterstock: Curly Pat, Magnia, Markovka, Ms.Moloko, Orfeev,
pockygallery, Sashatigar, Zabrotskaya Larisa

Printed in the United States of America in Stevnes Point, Wisconsin .
032015   008824WZF15

Table of Contents

Life on Earth

What does it mean to be alive and active? A group of students running the mile in gym class is certainly active. So is a dog chasing after a ball. And plants inside a greenhouse with their leaves angled toward the sun are living too.

But what about the green stuff growing on rocks at the bottom of lakes? Or that gallon of milk that's starting to smell funny? What processes are responsible for the way our planet works? What invisible things are happening to the world around us?

Dive into experiments and explore some of the principles behind our living Earth using ordinary household items. Some of these experiments may require an adult's help. But you can do most of them on your own. If things get messy, just remember to clean up. It's time to roll up your sleeves and get those hands dirty!

Into the Darkness

Plants are essential to life on Earth. Like you, plants also need food to live. They have a unique way of getting food. Through **photosynthesis**, most plants are able to make their own food. **Chlorophyll** is very important to the process. Chlorophyll is also what gives plants their green color. But what happens when chlorophyll doesn't get any sunlight? You can discover the answer to this question using a few simple supplies.

Cycle of Plant Life

Plants need light, water, and **carbon dioxide** for photosynthesis to take place. During photosynthesis plants release oxygen into the air. That's where animals and humans get oxygen to breathe. When animals and humans breathe in oxygen, they breathe out carbon dioxide and water. This process is known as **respiration** and is the opposite of photosynthesis. Together they form a cycle that supports most life on Earth.

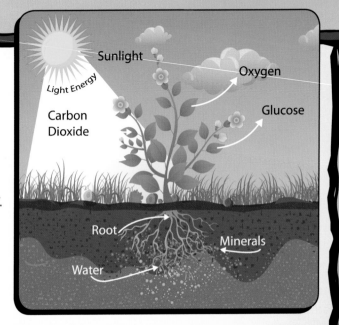

Sunlight

Oxygen

Light Energy

Glucose

Carbon Dioxide

Root

Minerals

Water

6

What You Do

1. Buy a small houseplant or choose one already in your house. Make sure it has large leaves.

2. Place the plant in a sunny window.

3. Wrap black construction paper around one leaf of the plant. Tape it in place.

4. Water the plant according to the directions that came with the plant.

5. Remove the construction paper after one week.

How does the leaf you covered look compared to the other leaves? How did the construction paper affect the chlorophyll?

What You Need

indoor plant with large leaves

black construction paper

tape

water

photosynthesis–the process by which green plants make their food

chlorophyll–the green substance in plants that uses light to make food from carbon dioxide and water

carbon dioxide–a colorless, odorless gas that people and animals breathe out

respiration–the process of taking in oxygen and sending out carbon dioxide

7

"Watering" Plants

Plants grow differently depending on their **environments**. Soil type, temperature, sunlight, and water are all factors that can affect plant growth. But what about the type of water? Houseplants are usually watered from a sink. Outdoor plants often survive on rainwater. Maybe water isn't the only thing that can make a plant grow. What would happen if you gave a plant a drink meant for people, such as soda or orange juice?

environment–the natural world of the land, water, and air

What You Do

1. Use your pen to poke a small hole in the bottom of each cup.

2. Fill each cup about halfway with potting soil.

3. Put three seeds into each cup. Follow the seed packet's instructions about how deeply to plant each seed.

4. Write labels for two cups to show what type of liquid you will use on each plant. The third cup should be labeled "water." Tape the labels onto the cups.

5. Set the cups onto the tray. Put the tray in a sunny windowsill.

6. Water each plant with ⅓ cup (80 milliliters) liquid for each labeled cup.

7. Continue to water each cup every other day with ⅓ cup (80 mL) liquid. If the cups spill out a lot of liquid, you can reduce the amount.

8. Take notes about when a plant first appears in each cup.

   What differences do you notice between the plants? How did the liquid you chose for each cup affect the plants' growth? Were there any cups where no plants grew at all?

9

Compost Jars

If you've ever gardened, you may have heard of **compost**. It is made from organic matter such as leaves, grass clippings, fruit peels, or coffee grounds. Compost is created when bacteria and fungi cause the materials to rot and break down. The process is an important part of the food chain. Once a plant dies, something has to help that plant **decompose**. Then it becomes compost, which helps new life grow. Many people spread compost in their gardens to help plants grow better.

compost—mixture of rotted leaves, vegetables, manure, and other items that are added to soil to make it richer

decompose—to rot or decay

Not everything can be composted. Some things take too long to break down. What items break down the fastest? What conditions help this process? Beware, compost can get stinky!

How long to decompose?

Banana peel ➡	3–4 weeks
Cardboard ➡	2 months
Plastic bags ➡	Between months and hundreds of years
Aluminum can ➡	200 years
Disposable diapers ➡	500 years
Styrofoam ➡	1 million years

FACT

From 20 to 30 percent of what we throw in the trash can be composted. Composting is good because it helps create healthy soil and reduces trash in landfills. Some people have compost bins in their backyards.

What You Do

What You Need

soil collected from a yard, playground, or field

3 clear jars or bottles of a similar shape and size

fruit scraps (banana peel, orange peel, apple core, etc.)

2-inch (5-centimeter) piece of Styrofoam or plastic

1 piece of paper, torn into strips

measuring spoons

water

spoon or fork

sunny windowsill

pen and paper or notebook for taking notes

1. Add soil to each jar or bottle until each is half full.

2. Put fruit scraps in one jar, the piece of Styrofoam or plastic in another, and a few strips of paper in the third.

3. Add 1 tablespoon (15 mL) water to each jar. Mix everything together.

4. Leave the lids off and place the jars in a sunny windowsill in a well-**ventilated** room. Make notes about what you see every day. Include information such as the size, shape, and color of any objects you can see as the mixture begins to turn into compost.

5. After one week, add 1 more tablespoon (15 mL) water to each jar and mix the contents. Write down any changes you notice to the objects.

6. Continue the experiment for another several weeks if you wish. Repeat step 5 after each week.

You should see that the fruit scraps and paper start to decompose, while the plastic or Styrofoam does not. Why is this? What is the connection between what you observed and why people might recycle?

ventilate–to allow fresh air into a place and to send stale air out

How Fast Do Things Decompose in Landfills?

For something to decompose, it needs to be in certain conditions. Bacteria, fungi, water, sunlight, and heat all make decomposition possible. But many landfills are packed too tightly for the conditions to be present. That's why items in a landfill might decompose much more slowly than they do in your windowsill experiment. Researchers from Michigan State University decided to dig into a landfill and look at old trash. They found grass clippings and several hot dogs that were more than 30 years old. They even found a 30-year-old newspaper that was still readable.

Earth's Layers

The top layers of Earth are called **sedimentary** layers. They are like a book that tells the history of life on our planet. The sediment that makes up the layers can be as small as a piece of dirt or as large as a boulder.

Sedimentation can be a helpful process. When rivers move sediment downstream, the sediment often adds good **nutrients** to the soil. That's why the land beside rivers is often great farmland. Now it's your turn to experiment with sedimentation!

sediment–tiny bits of rock, shells, plants, sand, and minerals that settle to the bottom of a liquid

nutrient–a substance needed by a living thing to stay healthy

What You Do

1. Cut the top off the plastic bottle so it has a wide opening through which to pour particles.

2. Drop in equal amounts of each of the three natural particles you collected.

3. Pour water into the bottle until it covers the particles and stops about 4 inches (10 cm) above the particles.

4. Set the bottle in a sunny window. Stir the materials with the plastic spoon or stick so they are well-mixed. Be careful not to spill.

5. Make notes about what the particles look like after one minute, 30 minutes, and 24 hours.

   Look at the layers formed inside the bottle. Which particles settled to the bottom the fastest? Which ended up on top? How do the weight and size of each particle type influence how quickly the particles settle to the bottom?

What You Need

scissors

clean, empty plastic bottle or milk jug

1 cup (240 mL) each of three natural particles of different sizes, such as sand, dirt, small pebbles, or rocks

water

sunny window

plastic spoon or stick

pen and paper or notebook for taking notes

clock or timer

15

Make Your Own Fossils!

Fossils have helped us learn much of what we know about past life on Earth. They show us how long different life forms have been around and how those life forms lived in the past. They can even teach us about plants and animals that no longer exist. Fossils can also tell us about what the planet used to look like.

fossil–the remains or traces of plants and animals that are preserved as rock

Sometimes fossils are the remains of living things, such as bones, teeth, and wood. Fossils can also be the imprint of something, such as a foot or a leaf that is no longer there. How are fossils made? Make your own and find out!

What You Do

What You Need

½ cup (120 mL) used, wet coffee grounds

½ cup (120 mL) cold coffee

½ cup (120 mL) salt

1 cup (240 mL) flour

waxed paper or parchment paper

4 different objects, such as a leaf, a twig, a small toy, or your foot

1. Mix together the coffee grounds, coffee, salt, and flour. It should form a doughlike substance.

2. Divide the dough into four chunks.

3. Flatten each chunk onto a sheet of waxed paper or parchment paper.

4. Press one object into each of your flattened chunks of dough. Then remove the object.

5. Let the mixture dry overnight.

6. Now show your fossil imprints to your family or friends!

Can your family or friends tell what object made each fossil? One thousand years from now, what could your fossil imprints tell about the place where you live?

Paleontology

For decades **paleontologists** have used tools such as hammers, picks, and brushes to clear away dirt and dig up fossils. Paleontologists also use advanced tools such as microscopes and computers. Fossils can tell us information about what the planet was like thousands of years ago. Fossils also allow scientists to predict how the environment will change and impact life in the future.

paleontologist—scientist who studies fossils

Homemade Salt Flats

Salt flats are big, flat stretches of land covered with salt and other **minerals**. Salt flats are the result of **evaporation** from a former body of water. This would be similar to plugging your sink and then filling it with water. The water can't drain away, so it stays there until it evaporates. In a salt flat, while the water is evaporating, salt and minerals that are in the water stay behind.

Salt flats are an example of how the living Earth is always changing. The Bonneville Salt Flats in Utah were once a lake as big as Lake Michigan. And it's possible that as weather patterns change, a salt flat could flood and become a lake once again. Try to make your own miniature salt flat using a few common items!

mineral–a solid substance found in nature that is produced by natural processes

evaporate–to change from a liquid to a vapor or a gas

What You Do

What You Need

large mixing bowl

spoon for stirring

measuring cups

salt

hot water

measuring spoons

baking soda

potting soil

glass baking dish

pen and paper or notebook
  for taking notes

1. In a bowl, stir ½ cup (120 mL) salt into 1 cup (240 mL) hot water until the salt dissolves.

2. Add 1 tablespoon (15 mL) baking soda and 1 tablespoon (15mL) soil. Stir again.

3. Pour the mixture into a glass baking dish. Let the dish sit for a few days until the water has evaporated. Take notes on the color and **texture** of the mixture.

4. Repeat step 1 again. Pour the new mixture on top of the dried mixture. Let it dry for a few days.

5. Repeat steps 1 and 2, using ½ cup (120 mL) salt, 1 cup (240 mL) hot water, ⅓ cup (80 mL) baking soda, and ⅓ cup (80 mL) soil. Pour the new mixture on top of the dried mixture. Let it dry for a few more days. Take notes on the color and texture of all of the layers.

6. Repeat two or three more times with different amounts of baking soda and soil each time. Take notes about the look and texture of each layer.

What do you notice about the look and feel of each layer? Why do you think nothing grows in a salt flat?

texture–the way something feels when you touch it

A Watery Planet

About 97 percent of the water on Earth is salt water. It is important for the many creatures that live in the oceans. Humans and many other animals, however, need freshwater to survive. But many countries have experienced water shortages in recent years. Some parts of the United States, including California and Arizona, are having water shortages. One potential solution is to use **desalination** to turn salt water into freshwater.

Some countries—including Saudi Arabia, Israel, and Singapore—already use desalination. Now you can see how this process works without leaving your house!

FACT

Desalination is not an environmentally friendly process. A desalination plant uses three times the amount of energy than a regular water treatment plant does. It also requires chemicals that may harm the ocean.

What You Do

What You Need

- measuring cups
- water
- 2 cereal bowls
- measuring spoons
- table salt
- spoon for stirring
- drinking straw
- clay
- large mixing bowl
- plastic wrap
- large rubber band
- small rock
- sunny windowsill

1. Pour 2 cups (475 mL) water into a cereal bowl. Add 2 tablespoons (30 mL) salt and stir until salt is **dissolved**.

2. With the straw, take a small sip of water and spit it out. It should taste salty. Don't swallow!

3. Flatten a piece of clay and put it in the bottom of the mixing bowl.

4. Pour the salt water into the mixing bowl until the water is about 1 inch (2.5 cm) high.

5. Place the second cereal bowl into the mixing bowl and press it into the clay. The cereal bowl should be higher than the water but below the top of the mixing bowl. The cereal bowl should be dry inside.

6. Wrap plastic wrap over the top of the mixing bowl. Let the plastic wrap sag a little into the bowl but not touch the water or bowl. Hold the plastic wrap in place by wrapping the rubber band around the mixing bowl just below the rim.

7. Place the rock on the center of the plastic wrap so the plastic wrap dips toward the cereal bowl.

8. Place the mixing bowl in a sunny windowsill for a day or two.

You should notice some water has collected in the cereal bowl. Take a sip of this water. What do you taste?

desalinate–the process of removing salt from water

dissolve–to seem to disappear when mixed with liquid

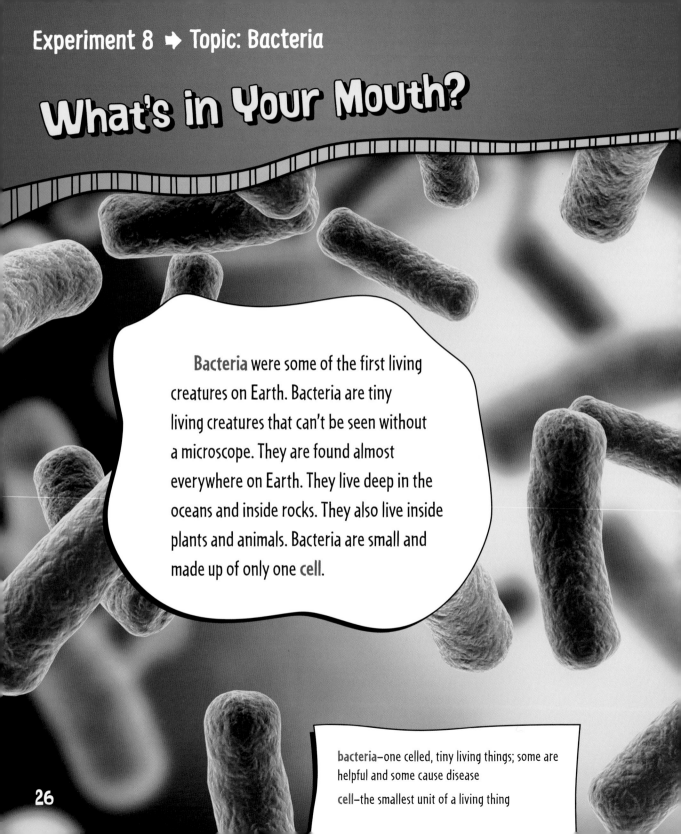

What's in Your Mouth?

Bacteria were some of the first living creatures on Earth. Bacteria are tiny living creatures that can't be seen without a microscope. They are found almost everywhere on Earth. They live deep in the oceans and inside rocks. They also live inside plants and animals. Bacteria are small and made up of only one **cell**.

bacteria–one celled, tiny living things; some are helpful and some cause disease

cell–the smallest unit of a living thing

Some bacteria are helpful to people. We have good bacteria that live inside our bodies and help us process food. Other kinds of bacteria are used to help ripen cheese and make medicine.

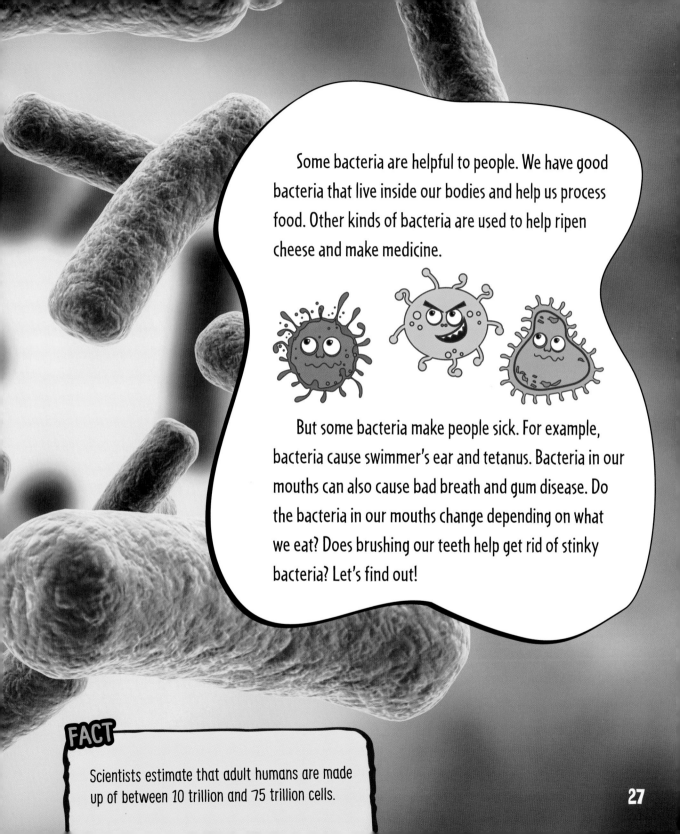

But some bacteria make people sick. For example, bacteria cause swimmer's ear and tetanus. Bacteria in our mouths can also cause bad breath and gum disease. Do the bacteria in our mouths change depending on what we eat? Does brushing our teeth help get rid of stinky bacteria? Let's find out!

FACT

Scientists estimate that adult humans are made up of between 10 trillion and 75 trillion cells.

What You Do

1. Label the agar plates "control," "candy," and "bread."

2. Brush your teeth with toothpaste, and rinse your mouth with water.

3. Rub a cotton swab against the inside of your cheek. Then wipe it across the agar plate marked "control" so your saliva forms a line down the plate.

4. Eat the piece of candy.

5. Repeat step 3 using the agar plate marked "candy."

6. Brush your teeth and rinse your mouth again. Then eat the piece of bread.

7. Repeat step 3 using the agar plate marked "bread."

8. Put the lids on the agar plates, tape them shut, and put them in a dark cupboard.

9. After 24 hours look at each plate and make notes about what you see. Include information such as the number and size of any visible bacteria growth.

10. Make notes again after two days, three days, and four days.

What do you see in each plate? You should see bacteria growing. The dish marked "candy" should have the most bacteria. What does this suggest about the role of sugar in helping bacteria grow? Why is it important to brush your teeth?

Safety First!

Always keep the agar plates taped closed. When it is time to throw them away, seal them in a plastic bag and throw them in the garbage.

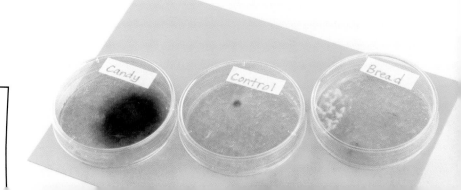

agar plate–a small clear dish filled with a gel that helps microscopic things grow

Extraordinary Earth

You don't need fancy laboratory equipment to understand
how the natural world works. Life on Earth involves
amazing cycles of growth and decay. If you know where
to look, every day brings you into contact with these living
processes. From dead leaves to young plants to desert
sands, the planet is changing and living, just like we are.

Glossary

agar plate (AH-gahr PLAYT)—a small clear dish filled with a gel that helps microscopic things grow

bacteria (bak-TEER-ee-uh)—one celled, tiny living things; some are helpful and some cause disease

carbon dioxide (KAHR-buhn dy-AHK-syd)—a colorless, odorless gas that people and animals breathe out

cell (SEL)—the smallest unit of a living thing

chlorophyll (KLOR-uh-fil)—the green substance in plants that uses light to make food from carbon dioxide and water

compost (KOM-pohst)—mixture of rotted leaves, vegetables, manure, and other items that are added to soil to make it richer

decompose (dee-kuhm-POHZ)—to rot or decay

desalinate (dee-SAL-uh-neyt)—the process of removing salt from water

dissolve (di-ZOLV)—to seem to disappear when mixed with liquid

environment (in-VY-ruhn-muhnt)—the natural world of the land, water, and air

evaporate (i-VA-puh-rayt)—to change from a liquid to a vapor or a gas

fossil (FAH-suhl)—the remains or traces of plants and animals that are preserved as rock

mineral (MIN-ur-uhl)—a solid substance found in nature that is produced by natural processes

nutrient (NOO-tree-uhnt)—a substance needed by a living thing to stay healthy

paleontologist (pale-ee-uhn-TOL-uh-jist)—scientist who studies fossils

photosynthesis (foh-toh-SIN-thuh-siss)—the process by which green plants make their food

respiration (ress-puh-RAY-shuhn)—the process of taking in oxygen and sending out carbon dioxide

sediment (SED-uh-muhnt)—tiny bits of rock, shells, plants, sand, and minerals that settle to the bottom of a liquid

texture (TEKS-chur)—the way something feels when you touch it

ventilate (VEN-tuh-layt)—to allow fresh air into a place and to send stale air out

Read More

Gray, Susan H. *Paleontology: The Study of Prehistoric Life.*
New York: Children's Press, 2012.

Iyer, Rani. *Endangered Energy: Investigating the Scarcity of Fossil Fuels.*
Endangered Earth. North Mankato, Minn.: Capstone Press, 2014.

Tomecek, Steve. *Dirtmeister's Nitty Gritty Planet Earth: All About Rocks, Minerals, Fossils, Earthquakes, Volcanoes, and Even Dirt!*
Washington, D.C.: National Geographic Society, 2015.

Yomtov, Nel. *Rocks and the People Who Love Them.* Adventures in Science.
Mankato, Minn.: Capstone Press, 2012.

Internet Sites

FactHound offers a safe, fun way to find Internet sites related to this book.
All of the sites on FactHound have been researched by our staff.

Here's all you do:
Visit *www.facthound.com*
Type in this code: **9781491448168**

Check out projects, games and lots more at
www.capstonekids.com

Index